BURN

BOOK

This Book Belongs to:

Made in the USA
Las Vegas, NV
02 October 2024

96111592R00036